brought decline, transforming the Cotswolds into a sleepy, rural time warp.

Today the Cotswolds remain an enchanted pastoral landscape of gently undulating grassy hills – panoramic distant views contrasting with mysterious wooded valleys. Although well-known beauty spots and quiet, undiscovered country are equally accessible by car, the Cotswold Way – a 100-mile (160-km) path traversing the entire region from north to south – remains the perfect way to see this delightful region.

2 A feature of the Cotswolds is its dry-stone walls, where skilfully-shaped interlocking stones require no mortar to keep them firmly in place for many years.

The Northern Cotswolds

The northern frontier of the Cotswolds lies just a few miles below Stratford-upon-Avon, and those travelling south across the Vale of Evesham will soon notice the higher ground ahead. Four of the region's most popular places – Chipping Campden, Broadway, Stow-on-the-Wold and Moreton-in-Marsh – are all situated in the north.

The Cotswold Way begins its long journey south at Chipping Campden, passing through lesser-visited, but equally fascinating places, such as Snowshill, Stanway, with its fine Jacobean manor house, the romantic ruin of Hailes Abbey and the neolithic longbarrow at Belas Knap with a sweeping view down towards historic Sudeley Castle.

There are equally fine views from Cleeve Hill and Dover's Hill, scene of the annual 'Cotswold Olympicks'.

A patchwork of well-kept fields and quiet beechwoods together with picture postcard cottages and splendid gardens collectively compose what for most people is the essential Cotswolds. Moreton-in-Marsh

3 A poppy field near the village of Broadway creates a bright splash of colour across the northern Cotswold landscape with sweeping views to distant horizons.

and Stow-on-the-Wold sit astride the Fosse Way, the old Roman road from Lincoln to Exeter, running arrow straight through Bourton-on-the-Water and Cirencester, much further south. Thus those with limited time can see a great deal within a short period – it all depends if your journey through the Cotswolds is in the fast or slow lane.

4 Hidcote Manor looks out over the Vale of Evesham on the northern fringes of the Cotswolds. Now owned by The National Trust, it has one of England's greatest gardens.

5 Kiftsgate Court was built in the late 19th century. Its beautiful garden lies on a steeply sloping site and is justly famous for its roses, particularly 'Kiftsgate' a rampant *rosa filipes*.

6 Dover's Hill, just north of Chipping Campden, is named after Sir Robert Dover who initiated 'the Cotswold Olympicks' during the reign of James I. Today the games are held annually on the weekend after the spring bank holiday.

8 The tall tower of St James's Church, Chipping Campden, overlooks the stylish lodges which are all that remain of Campden House, burnt down by Royalists during the Civil War in the mid-17th century.

9 The market hall at Chipping Campden dates from the early 17th century. The interior has a stone flag floor and a fine barrel-vaulted ceiling. 'Chipping' derives from the Saxon word *caepen*, meaning 'market'.

7 Sheep graze on grassy slopes above Chipping Campden. Once so large that they were called the Cotswold Lions, their wool provided the region with its original wealth and are still reared in large numbers throughout the area.

10 An abundance of flowers threatens to engulf this picturesque cottage in Broad Campden, a small village located just to the south of Chipping Campden.

11 Snowshill lies on a ridge with far-reaching north-easterly views. An archetypal Cotswold village, it has a long row of terraced stone cottages with distinctive dormer windows, running down a steeply sloping street.

12 The eccentric Charles Wade spent many years during the early 20th century restoring Snowshill Manor, then filling it with an extraordinary and eclectic collection ranging from samurai armour to musical instruments. It has a small, yet exquisite, garden, originally laid out by the Arts and Crafts architect, Mackay Hugh Baillie Scott.

13 Broadway Tower is a late 18th-century folly which stands on the summit of Broadway Beacon. William Morris and his friends used to stay here during their holidays. Reputedly, on a clear day, 13 counties can be seen from the top.

14 This intriguing statue of St George is attached to the wall of Wade's Cottage, alongside Snowshill Manor. Here, Charles Wade lived a spartan life for many years without the benefit of electricity.

15 The Gloucestershire and Warwickshire railway runs for several miles from Toddington and now reaches the outskirts of Cheltenham (at the racecourse) thanks to the restoration efforts of railway enthusiasts.

17 A pair of riders provide the only traffic in Stanton, a pretty village with a pleasing mixture of stone and half-timbered period houses, together with a medieval wayside cross.

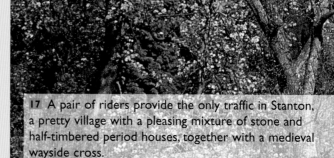

16 The evocative ruins of Hailes Abbey, originally a Cistercian foundation, initiated in the mid-13th century by Richard, Earl of Cornwall, in gratitude for surviving a storm at sea when returning from the Crusades. It was closed on the orders of King Henry VIII on Christmas Eve 1539.

18 The village of Stanway in early spring. It has a Jacobean manor house with a recently-restored Baroque water garden which contains an impressive 21-metre (70-feet) high fountain and a waterfall.

19 A ruined tithe barn provides an attractive backdrop for the lily pond at romantic Sudeley Castle, once the home of Catherine Parr, King Henry VIII's sixth wife, who is buried in the chapel in the grounds of the castle.

20 A distant view of Sudeley Castle, which was besieged during the Civil War and then left derelict for almost 200 years. Restored in Victorian times, it today houses a superb collection of paintings and furniture.

21 One of 40 highly unusual gargoyles on the exterior walls of the magnificent parish church of St Peter at Winchcombe, once the ancient capital of the Saxon kingdom of Mercia.

22 Vineyard Street in Winchcombe owes its name to the days when wine was produced in the area. Its enterprising citizens also grew tobacco until prohibited from doing so by an Act of Parliament.

23 This attractive house between Chipping Campden and Moreton-in-Marsh typifies the vernacular nature of Cotswold architecture: local stone, steeply-pitched thick tiled roof and mullioned dormer windows.

24 The Cotswold Farm Park is located close to the intriguingly named village of Guiting Power. The farm is the nation's major rare breeds centre.

25 Sezincote is India come to the Cotswolds. Its original owner had made a fortune in the East India Company during the 18th century.

26 Stow-on-the-Wold viewed across a wooded valley. Its status as the highest town in the Cotswolds prompts the old rhyme, 'Stow-on-the-Wold where the wind blows cold'.

27 Here seen through an elegant wrought iron gate, Stow-on-the-Wold has an extensive market square and a market cross. Every year the town continues to hold large horse fairs during May and October.

28 Snow covers an ancient farm cart and the roofs of the cottages in Upper Slaughter. In the winter months the Cotswolds can acquire a totally different type of beauty.

29 A ford crosses the river in Upper Slaughter, a village with a lovely Tudor manor. The word 'slaughter' in Saxon means 'a muddy place,' not a very romantic term for somewhere so attractive.

30 At nearby Lower Slaughter, the River Eye flows through the centre of the village, crossed by a series of low stone bridges, with traditional Cotswold cottages lining its banks.

31 The Cotswold Way offers around nine days' fairly gentle walking through very beautiful countryside. In the northern region, it passes through places such as Broadway, Stanton, Stanway, Hailes Abbey and Winchcombe.

32 Bourton House at Bourton-on-the-Hill is a handsome 18th-century building with an exceptional garden which is constantly being developed. It includes a knot garden, unusual statuary, a potager (kitchen garden) plus outstanding herbaceous borders.

33 Bourton-on-the-Water, probably the most popular place in the Cotswolds, has a variety of attractions including Birdland, the Cotswold Motor Museum and this superb model village.

34 This road sign at Great Tew somehow symbolizes the laid-back, relaxed pace of life in the Cotswolds.

SLOW! KITTENS

36 The River Windrush flows through the centre of Bourton-on-the-Water, crossed by a series of low ornamental bridges.

37 Just outside Chipping Norton stands the striking chimney of Bliss Mill which remained a tweed factory until 1980 and has since been converted into apartments.

35 East of Moreton-in-Marsh stand the enigmatic Rollright Stones, said by legend to be a king and his army turned to stone by a local witch, but more likely to be a Bronze Age stone circle and burial ground.

The Central Cotswolds

This region is one of infinite contrast. In the east lies the upper navigational limit of the River Thames at the pretty little town of Lechlade, with its distinctive needle-spire church. Not far away is idyllic Kelmscott Manor, Elizabethan home of William Morris, Vanbrugh's magnificent baroque Blenheim Palace and the medieval clapper bridge which connects the pretty villages of Eastleach Turville and Eastleach Martin.

The landscape is primarily open in the east, large fields divided by distinctive dry-stone walls, growing more wooded to the west. In autumn here, the colours are fabulous – a perfect time to visit. In the extreme west stands the elegant Regency spa town of Cheltenham, present-day venue of the internationally renowned Cheltenham Gold Cup, an annual event that sees all Ireland come to the races.

Between these limits the essentially flat ground rises imperceptibly westwards, passing well-known places such as Burford

38 Leckhampton Hill lies on the western escarpment of the Cotswolds, looking out over the town of Cheltenham and beyond. To the north is Cleeve Hill, or Cleeve Cloud as it is otherwise known, the highest point in the Cotswolds. To the south, Ermine Street, an old Roman road, runs in a virtually straight line past Cirencester and on to Swindon.

and Bibury together with a host of traditional, close-knit farming communities, and the magical Slad Valley, where the poet Laurie Lee discovered sex and cider with Rosie. The ground then falls away dramatically into the valley of the River Severn, forming a steep escarpment with breathtaking views all the way to Wales.

39 Every spring bank holiday, Cooper's Hill near Birdlip sees the Great Cheese Rolling Race, where competitors pursue giant 'cheeses' at high speed down a very steep slope.

40 At first sight the Devil's Chimney appears to be natural, yet this slender stone column is the result of quarrying. Situated by the Cotswold Way, it poses a tempting challenge to rock climbers. However the wreath at its base provides a grim warning.

41 The elegant Regency Promenade at Cheltenham was originally built in 1818 and remains little altered from those halcyon days when the nobility came to take the waters in this fashionable spa town.

42 The fountain in Cheltenham's Promenade represents a copy of the world famous Trevi Fountain which is located in Rome.

43 Benedictine monks at Prinknash Abbey, a modern foundation established in the early part of the 20th century. Here the monks are producing incense, sold in the abbey shop and worldwide.

44 Painswick's Rococo Gardens are famous for their snowdrops in early spring, carpeting the woods in great profusion. These remarkable gardens were originally laid out in the mid-18th century and today are being restored to their former glory.

45 Prinknash Abbey, on the Cotswold scarp just south of Gloucester, features a bird park and is justly famous for its distinctive dark grey pewter-ware.

46 Painswick is famous for its churchyard. The slender church spire, so characteristic of the Cotswolds, looks down on highly ornate tombstones among colonnades of ancient yew trees, beautifully clipped.

47 Painswick's splendid half-timbered post office dates back to the Middle Ages when the town was an exceedingly affluent woollen cloth producer.

49 Bisley is another unspoilt, pretty little village located in quiet countryside running due east of Stroud.

50 Misarden Park stands high on a hill overlooking the Golden Valley, east of Stroud. It possesses a superb garden partially laid out by Sir Edward Lutyens, who also carried out alterations and additions to the original Tudor house.

48 Slad was the childhood home of the author Laurie Lee. His youthful memories are reflected in his classic book, *Cider with Rosie*. The village is to be found in the lovely valley running northwards from Stroud.

51 The 12th-century font in the church of St Peter at Rendcomb is carved with the figures of eleven of Christ's apostles, the space for Judas remaining blank.

52 Duntisbourne Leer is one of four small hamlets named after the Dunt Brook which runs through the beautiful countryside north-east of Cirencester. Here the brook flows across the street. Mind you don't disturb the ducks!

53 Duntisbourne Rouse has an ancient isolated chapel overlooking a heavily wooded valley. It has a Saxon nave and a Norman chancel, the modest bell tower being added in the Tudor era.

54 Bibury is renowned for Arlington Row, a cluster of former weavers' cottages overlooking a water meadow called Rack Isle, where wool was once hung out to dry. Arlington Row is now the property of The National Trust.

55 The Swan Hotel at Bibury, a place that William Morris once described as 'the most beautiful village in all England.'

56 An unlikely scene: huge rhinoceros graze quietly with zebras at the Cotswold Wildlife Park, near Burford. The park has a large variety of animals together with an aquarium and an insect house.

57 This dovecote stands close to the ruins of Minster Lovell Hall, Lord Lovell's 15th-century manor house, which has a charming setting on the banks of the River Windrush, east of Burford.

58 Burford's main street slopes downhill to an old bridge over the River Windrush and is flanked by rows of exceptional period houses. Some interesting 15th-century almshouses are to be found close to the church. The minor road from Burford to Northleach along the Windrush Valley is one of the loveliest routes in the Cotswolds.

59 Cotswold Woollen Weavers at Firkins, near Burford, is a working weaving mill in an 18th-century barn, with a millshop and an exhibition gallery.

60 When 'Capability' Brown created the lake at Blenheim Palace as part of his landscaped park he half-submerged Sir John Vanbrugh's massive bridge. In the background is Vanbrugh's baroque masterpiece, conceived in the early part of the 18th century.

61 An aerial view of the north front of Blenheim Palace, Queen Anne's reward to her friend, the 1st Duke of Marlborough, after he decisively defeated the French at the Battle of Blenheim in 1704. Winston Churchill was born here in 1874. Today Blenheim is the home of the 11th Duke of Marlborough.

62 The spectacular water terrace at Blenheim Palace was created by Achille Duchene for the 9th Duke in the early part of the 20th century and echoes Andre le Notre's *parterre d'eau* at Versailles.

63 Woodstock lies at the entrance to Blenheim Palace, a small town of considerable charm with an interesting variety of shops, eating places and popular hotels.

64 Ancient Keble's Bridge links the twin villages of Eastleach Turville and Eastleach Martin. It is named after John Keble, the famous 19th-century poet and theologian, who was once curate here.

65 Riders in Eastleach Turville, a small hamlet south of Burford, consisting of very attractive houses of Cotswold stone.

66 Wild flowers flourish at Chedworth. Here a Roman villa dating from AD 120 lay preserved for centuries under layers of mud until discovered by chance in 1864. The villa, with its superb mosaics, is now owned by The National Trust.

The Southern Cotswolds

This is an almost secret Cotswolds, not nearly so well known as its northern counterparts. This is particularly true of the south western corner. Low-profile villages like Ozleworth and Easton Grey lie quietly in exquisite countryside where cock pheasants strut cheekily down deserted lanes and the inns have intriguing names like the Cat & Custard, the Rattlebone and the Trouble House.

The Southern Cotswolds are Royalist territory – Prince Charles, Princess Anne and Prince and Princess Michael of Kent all have houses in this enchanting part of England. This is the land of the horse, with the royals regularly playing polo near Cirencester, a town originally built by the Romans. Two of the biggest international horse trials take place annually at Badminton and

67 This low bridge takes the road over the River Coln into Fairford. This little gem of a town has the magnificent church of St Mary, which contains the only complete set of medieval narrative glass anywhere in England.

Gatcombe Park and in some parts of the countryside horses seem to outnumber motor cars.

In the 19th century, members of the Arts and Crafts movement established a community at Sapperton, where like-minded craftsmen lived and worked together. Today, nearby Rodmarton Manor is a show-house for their work. In complete contrast the Cotswold Water Park, near Cricklade, is Britain's largest water-sports centre.

The Cotswold Way finishes at the west door of Bath Abbey, a fitting place to end the journey through the Cotswolds.

68 Tiddles the Cat is unusually commemorated in the churchyard of St Mary's at Fairford.

69 This statue of Old Father Thames lies alongside St John's Lock at Lechlade, the furthest navigable part of the River Thames. Once important to commercial traffic, the river here is now very popular with pleasure craft.

70 Originally an Elizabethan farmhouse, Kelmscott Manor was for 25 years the idyllic country home of William Morris. Today it is full of his work, together with that of his Pre-Raphaelite friends and colleagues in the Arts and Crafts movement.

71 Kelmscott has a magical garden, containing this vine-covered pergola, colourful herbaceous borders, together with barns, dovecote and a meadow running down to the upper reaches of the River Thames.

73 This statue of a boy riding a dolphin is in Harold Peto's water garden at Buscot Park.

72 The late 18th-century Buscot Park near Lechlade possesses a magnificent art collection with paintings by Rembrandt, Gainsborough and the Pre-Raphaelites.

74 Cirencester was first established by the Romans and at one time was the second largest town in England. Its great wealth as a wool town during the Middle Ages is reflected in the magnificent parish church of St John the Baptist.

75 Cirencester Park is a regular venue for games of polo, often with royal participants. Polo is an increasingly popular sport in the Cotswolds and is also played at Westonbirt and Ladyswood.

77 Chavenage Manor is hidden away in a little-visited part of the Cotswolds near Tetbury. Only two families have ever owned the Elizabethan house, which has a hall, minstrel gallery, fine period furniture and tapestries.

76 This Roman mosaic head is housed in the Corinium Museum at Cirencester which also boasts a turfed Roman amphitheatre.

78 The Gatcombe Horse Trials, a three-day event featuring the British Open Championships, takes place every year on HRH The Princess Royal's extensive estate near Minchinhampton. The world's top riders and horses compete.

79 Westonbirt, considered to be the nation's finest arboretum, is now owned by the Forestry Commission, having originally been planted by Robert Holford in 1829, employing plant hunters in North America and the Orient. Today it contains 18,000 trees covering 600 acres (240ha) of ground.

80 An ancient arched bridge crosses the River Avon at Easton Royal, a delightful little village tucked away in a secluded valley just north of Malmesbury.

81 The Market House at Tetbury dates from the mid-17th century and continues to be used for regular markets. Tetbury is also a popular centre of the antiques trade.

82 Stout Tuscan pillars support the Market House in Tetbury. Each spring bank holiday Monday the town hosts the woolsack races, when intrepid relay teams carry a sack weighing 48lbs (22kg) up the daunting slope of Gumstool Hill.

83 The carving around the south porch of Malmesbury Abbey displays Norman craftsmanship at its finest in a town whose charter was originally granted by King Alfred the Great.

84 Malmesbury Abbey once possessed a spire that was considerably taller than that of Salisbury Cathedral – but it collapsed towards the end of the 15th century. The town also has an impressive medieval market cross.

85 St Nicholas Church at Ozleworth, hidden away in a secluded valley to the north-east of Wotton-under-Edge, has a highly unusual hexagonal Norman tower.

86 In a remote valley setting above Dursley is the romantic Tudor manor house of Owlpen with a formal garden dating back to the 16th century. Close by are a 17th-century courthouse, an 18th-century mill and a Victorian church.

87 Wotton-under-Edge in the depths of winter with a pristine carpet of dazzlingly white snow under a bright blue sky, conditions which can often happen at this time of year in the Cotswolds.

88 The internationally famous Badminton Horse Trials, consisting of dressage, cross country and show jumping, take place annually in the grounds of Badminton House. Only the very best horses and riders are permitted to compete, the jumps on the 4½ mile (7km) cross-country course being particularly fearsome.

89 Horton Court is a Cotswold manor house with an attached medieval hall. The Renaissance loggia in the grounds was inspired by the Tudor owner's trip to Rome to negotiate King Henry VIII's divorce from Catherine of Aragon.

90 High on the ridge above North Nibley stands the Tyndale Monument, a memorial to the first man to translate the New Testament into English – he was subsequently burnt at the stake as a heretic.

91 Castle Combe in Wiltshire is a prime candidate for the most beautiful village in the Cotswolds, with unspoilt former weavers' cottages running down to the river.

92 The classic view down the main street of Castle Combe from the covered market cross. The village was once renowned for its distinctive red and white cloth which it produced in the 15th century.